AFRICAN SPIRITUALITY

BY: GLORIA ADWOA AMOANIMAA KONADU (STORIES BY AERAYE).

TABLE OF CONTENTS

TABLE OF CONTENTS

YOU, THEY WILL NOT STOP/ STOP IT FOR YOU WILL NOT

LIKE IT IF IT IS DONE TO YOU.

<u>Beginning</u>

This book is being written out of a need that I feel should be brought to light that African Spirituality is real and a true form of worshipping GOD, IT CAN BE FOUND IN THE CHRISTIAN BIBLE IN EXODUS CH. 20 VS. 22-25, IT SAYS: Then the LORD said to Moses, "Tell the Israelites this: 'You have seen for yourselves that I have spoken to you from heaven:(A) 23 Do not make any gods to be alongside me;(B) do not make for yourselves gods of silver or gods of gold.(C)

24 "'Make an altar(D) of earth for me and sacrifice on it your burnt offerings(E) and fellowship offerings, your sheep and goats and your cattle. Wherever I cause my name(F) to be honored, I will come to you and bless(G) you. 25 If you make an altar of stones for me, do not build it with dressed stones, for you will defile it if you use a tool(H) on it.   I want to ask anyone who is of different spiritual or religious belief to take this information with a new look and insight.

It states in the bible that Genesis Chapter 1, Vs 2, it says "And the earth was without form, and void; and darkness was upon the face of the deep. And the Spirit of God (Holy Spirit) moved upon the face of the waters; So to my understanding, the HOLY

SPIRIT is like the companion of GOD or "Better Half" of

GOD. The reason for me to say this is that, creation came about

because of GOD and the HOLY SPIRIT. I believe the HOLY

SPIRIT was doing GOD's work also in the creation of the world

and all that was created by The CREATOR.

To start the book of what I believe is the Asante people or AKAN

people of GHANA, I cannot go into the history of the AKAN's but

what I believe, the ONE TRUE GOD has made me realise is what I

want others to read, listen and take some part of knowledge and

live a better life.

Our first history of a priest in the African Spiritualism in the

Asante Region is of Okomfo Anokye. It is believed that he brough forth the GOLDEN STOOL from the sky and it is that which 8the

KING of ASANTE LAND sat on.

  In The beginning of creation, GOD was present and so was the

HOLY SPIRIT. Thus when one is praying to GOD, we say "Nyame

Agya, Nyame Oba, ne Nyame Homhom Kronkron (In the name of

THE FATHER,THE SON, AND THE HOLY SPIRIT)".

THE CREATOR of heaven and earth, created first the

earth{Asaase YAA=Y3n ara asaase (Our Own Earth) BOAFOWAA

} and then the man whom she is to be his help mate who controls

the universe is YAW= y3n ara wiase (Our Own World)

AGYEMANG.

Yaa BOAFOWAA because BOAFOWAA literally means Helper and so she is to help her counterpart in the responsibilities of taking care of the earth and his name is AGYEMANG because AGYEMANG Means to SAVE THE LAND OR TO TAKE THE LAND; he has authority over all the planets in the universe.

THE CREATOR gave the earth many minerals, Gold, gems, diamonds, rubies, crystals, pearls, Petrol, and many more..etc, and many more things. THE CREATOR also provided the earth with abundance of fresh waters and oceans, lakes, streams, etc. THE CREATOR gave the earth flora and fauna for creating medicines to cure many diseases and ailments for both men and women.

From there, THE CREATOR created other days and with each new day, a new man and woman was created, and so on and so forth.

Eg.. Adwoa and Kwadwo for Monday, Kwabena and Abena for Tuesday, Akua and Kwaku for Wednesday, Yaa and Yaw for

Thursday, Kofi and Afia for Friday, Kwame and Ama for Saturday and Finally, Akwasi and Akosua for Sunday.

I will like to explain what each of the day names given by the AKAN people of GHANA. It will only make sense in "Babble" :

11 Now the whole world had one language[A] and a common speech. 2 As people moved eastward,[a] they found a plain in Shinar[b][B] and settled there.

3 They said to each other, "Come, let's make bricks[C] and bake them thoroughly." They used brick instead of stone,[D] and tar[E] for mortar. 4 Then they said, "Come, let us build ourselves a city, with a tower that reaches to the heavens,[F] so that we may make a name[G] for ourselves; otherwise we will be scattered[H] over the face of the whole earth."[I]

5 But the LORD came down[J] to see the city and the tower the people were building. 6 The LORD said, "If as one people speaking

the same language[K] they have begun to do this, then nothing they plan to do will be impossible for them. 7 Come, let us[L] go down[M] and confuse their language so they will not understand each other."[N]

8 So the LORD scattered them from there over all the earth,[O] and they stopped building the city. 9 That is why it was called Babel[c][P]—because there the LORD confused the language[Q] of the whole world.[R] From there the LORD scattered[S] them over the face of the whole earth.

(The first language of humans as per the bible before "The Lord" changed our tongues given us different viewpoints and languages for GOD.)

ADWOA=   Anointing Deliverance Will Occur Always

KWADWO= Knows What Almighty Delivers When Omniscient.

Adwoa and Kwadwo are like water, when they rise in temperature is when they are upset but when cool, they are like life giving water

KWABENA = King Will Always Be Eternally Near Always OR Knowledge will abound brilliantly entirely now, always.

ABENA = Arise, believers Entertain New Avenues.

Kwabena and Abena have first love affection for their loved ones.

KWAKU= Kings Will Always Know Universe.

AKUA= Always Knows Universal Arivals.

Kwaku and Akua have kindness towards their loved ones.

YAA= Y3n Ara Asaase

YAW= Y3n Ara Wiase

Yaa and Yaw whom God gave governance of the earth and universe have love for the world and universe.

KOFI = Knowledge of Finance and Family Infinately.

AFIA= Always Finds Individuality Again.

Kofi and Afia usually shows in their own way love to those they love.

AMA= Always Maintain Abilities.

KWAME= Knowledge Will Always Maintain Eternally.

AMA and Kwame show love in through understanding in their own way.

AKWASI= Always Knows What Always Seems Impossible.

AKOSUA= Always Knows Omnipotent Saviours Understanding Also.

Akwasi and Akosua teaches their loved one's lessons to live by.

For communication to happen, GOD gave us all the abilities to speak and also to communicate long distance. THE CREATOR gave us psychic abilities to communicate with loved ones in case of travel. In the olden days, when there were no talking drums, smoke signals, wifi, telephones, telegraphs etc… we communicated psychically. Eg.. will be when you think of the person and ask the Holy Spirit with GOD'S

BLESSINGS and PERMISSION, and by HIS (GOD'S) WILL to allow communication to happen, AMEN, you say the persons name or think of the person then say a message to the person and through the power of the HOLY SPIRIT, The WIND will take it to the person via someone having a conversation, then the specific message you want the person to hear, the person will hear through the person walking by and talking or it can be a thought in the person whom you want the message to go to. For this Gift to be

bestowed onto you, You must not use it for evil, selfishness etc..

GOD also created with the earth many creatures and animals that

YAW AGYEMANG will manage.. The ones that GOD uses the most

by the AKANS to help in helping GOD'S work are

NANA ANANSE-THE SPIDER-WISDOM

GOD anointed ANANSE with wisdom and knowledge of many

things in the world for him to impart it on GOD'S children by

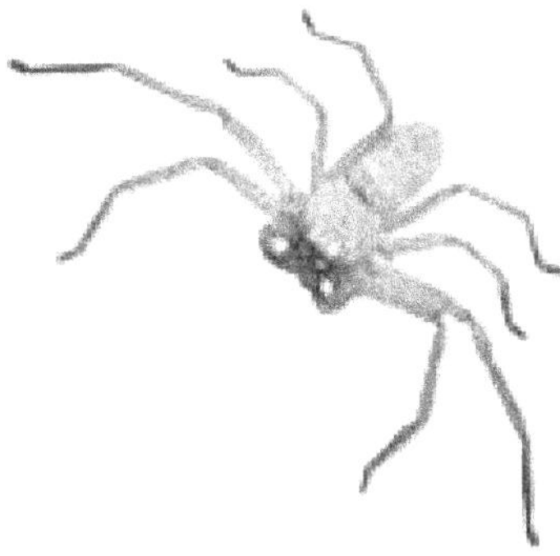

teaching them through SPIRITUAL means.

NANA ONKA (NANKA)-THE SERPENT-VINDICATIONThe

serpent can live in the water, on grass and in trees. So it is able to

see different views of the world that most people and animals or

creatures can't.

APAN-THE BAT To hear things in the dark that others may not

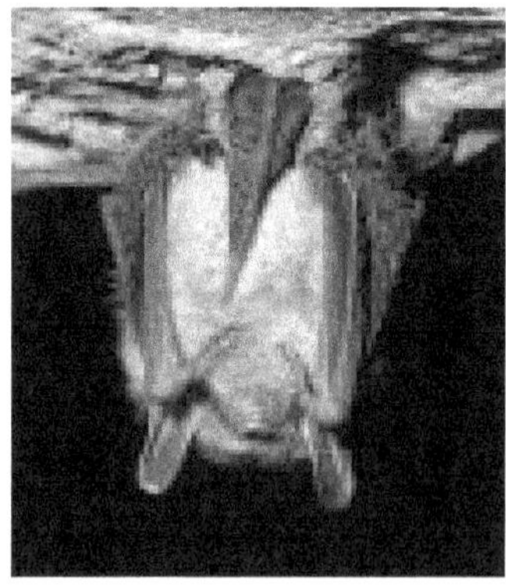

hear.

APETUO-THE OWL

To see things in the dark that others may not see.

OKODIE-EAGLE-VISION

To see far distances, fly (soar) higher

AKROMA-HAWK-SPEED-To strike faster into enemies

THE WIND(MFRAMA)-Communication

Which is how the HOLY SPIRIT travels to reach us. We ask the WIND to carry our thoughts, messages to the destination that the message needs to be or go.

<u>JUSTICE-</u>

In African Spirituality, the way to seek justice is to ask OboadiE (THE CREATOR), in an instance where someone has done you wrong or even if you are going through things that you may not see with your physical eyes, and you need help, look to GOD and pray this prayer

" Nyame a wo nim bibiara"

A, wo w) soro ni asaase so,

 Nsuo mu ni babiara"

S3 di3 nsuo tene w) wiase, a 3y3 kronkron no

Me de NSUO a 3w)..(Name of Country) i mu

Me sr3 wo, di m'as3m ma me

Biribi 3k)so a m'ntiasi3 na aboro me so

Me di NYAME DIN NE HOMHOM KRONKRON SR3 WO

BOA ME NA NOKWARE 3NDA DI

Y3 FR3 ME ………(then your name plus nicknames)"

If you have any additional names, add it on.

God, then state all your names,

"GOD who knows everything"

In the skies and on earth,

in the waters and on land"

I beg and plead with you,

Find out the truth of what I don't

Understand and I'm baffled by

I ASK YOU IN THE NAME OF GOD

THROUGH THE POWER OF THE

HOLY SPIRIT. As water flows in every

Part of THE WORLD, or (the country), please

let it

Purity and strength flow through me

and search my mind, heart, soul, spirit and

being to determine the truth of what is going

on and let GOD PASS THE JUDGMENT

AFTER TRUTH IS REVEALED".

Then you take(drink) water because it is pure and you ask the

country, in which you live in, eg.. Canada, then ask for the

SPIRITS in the water of that country to work through the

water and through your body. Let it search your whole body, mind, spirit, heart and soul, every crevice of your being let it pass through you then to the people whom you may know or may not know but through the SPIRIT, the WATER will work through whom ever will drink water in that said country till the truth of your problem or matter is revealed. When the TRUTH is revealed, GOD will see fit the punishment to give to the people or persons responsible for your pain, troubles, hurt, financial loss, etc. For the Judgement not to work, the

person will be reminded by GOD of his/her SINS AGAINST YOU, so they may rectify, apologise or fix the problem. How the people of the trials you've been through, has to apologise; they have to state their name, the reason why they did what they did and apologise if they can't find you after trying to find you then they should ask GOD to communicate the apology through the WINDS to you. Because it says in the bible in JOHN Chapter 8 vs. 32 "yes shall know the truth and the truth shall set you free".

PAPA NY3 WHEE A B)NI NSO NY3 WHEE(IF GOODNESS IS NOTHING, THEN BADNESS IS ALSO NOTHING).

The reason why water and egg is used is because the fluid of man blesses the egg of a woman in humans as well as all creatures and so they symbolize the beginning of life. It isn't good to use alcohol because alcohol dries up and kills living things and so to do proper "DUA BO" YOU will need water and egg to symbolize the beginning of life and then you add the alcohol only if you want your own justice instead of waiting for the Holy Spirit to work it's presence in the job in which you've taxed the Holy Spirit to do.

Also water is used because all living creatures have water as part of them and the whole world has in it water which we need to survive. Water moves from one place to another and discover things that we may not know. So if someone does you wrong follow

the directions given to find truth and justice because if

GOODNESS is NOTHING, then so is BADNESS because the

Spirit in the water through the HOLY SPIRIT will vindicate you.

TRUE,SPIRIT,SOUL,RIB,IDEAL MATE-

For the progression of the human race, THE CREATOR gave

everyone their Ideal,True,soul,rib mate. In all our lives, we may

not meet all the men and women that GOD has planned for our

lives, but there is a way in which you can be with the man or woman

who is supposed to be with you, if and when GOD PERMITS. There

are seven days in the week that THE CREATOR created. In the

AKAN CULTURE, the seven days, each have a different name

given to the boy and girl of the particular day.

As already talked about previously, Adwoa and Kwadwo, Kwabena and Abena, Kwaku and Akua, Yaw and Yaa, Kofi and Afia, Ama and Kwame and finally, Akwasi and Akosua.

In one's life, one may only meet their True, Ideal, Soul, Spirit, Rib Mate in the instance they start dating and it may lead to marriage whilst others will go through the whole week of men or women before finally getting whom GOD PLANNED FOR THEM. FOR example, A PERSON who has known four sexual partners meaning those that she's had intercourse with and have kissed five people but may only being in a relationship with one person. I will tell you why that one person that I believe is the real relationship that he or she might have had is the one person that they loved the most but gave up on him or her because he or she didn't want to hurt that person's future. But really that is the person that they should have been with, of all the people she had been with. if she was to count the days of the week of men she has been with it would be eg.. Kwabena, Kwaku, Kofi but she may have not been with Kwame or Yaw but the last two people I believe one of them through the week, one of them is her ideal mate. not the last, but through the week, she might have given up on the one person that she loved the most. To find your ideal, real, true, honest, spirit, soul rib mate God designed the program that is included as what we do every day without a thought like how a newborn child, when placed on her or his mother's chest try and go and find the Breast to try and eat, The AKAN'S will say (w) di na no pim pim " He or she is pounding his or her lips "looking for food to eat".) that's what a newborn baby does. That is what we do to search for our real, ideal, true, spirit, soul rib mate is licking our lips. Can one person tell me that they have never licked their lips? it is a certain method that THE CREATOR implanted so that when we meet somebody that we like we automatically LICK our lips. This is a method to search for that person. The real, true, ideal, rib, spiritual, soul mate whom you are to marry in the physical, that you will grow in health, wealth, family etc.. when you lick your lips. I have a poem that I've written, first say this poem:

ORAL STIMULATION;

Let my words

Enter your ears

Let it stimulate

Your soul to the core

When the vibrations of my sound (Voice)

Enters your tympanic membrane,

Let it stimulate you

Orally, Spiritually, Truthfully and Sexually.

After saying this poem, say this next poem along with it "LICK"

Let me lick my lips 1234

Think of the one i'm (you) are with 1234

Feel ORGASMIC, Truthful, Spiritual, Orally, Sexually,

1234

A lot or A little; 1234

Feel it and cum (Ejaculate), 1234

This may only happen when the person is your TRUE, REAL,

IDEAL, SOUL, SPIRIT, RIB MATE and with GOD'S PERMIT

through the HOLY SPIRIT. I ask GOD to permit only for

consenting Adults who knows either spiritually or physically what is being done, in THE HOLY SPIRT'S NAME AND BY THE WILL OF GOD, AMEN. If they don't know let them be awakened and know through the HOLY SPIRIT, by GOD'S WILL, Amen.

You may ask God through the Holy Spirit and through the Prophet whom you pray through; it could be Muhammad or it could be the son of GOD, Jesus, it could be Okomfo Anokye, it could anyone whom your religion permits for you to pray through to get to GOD. Asking god through The Holy Spirit to make the person that you are interested in feel orgasmic orgasm through the clitoris area for the woman or the G- spot, and for the man the tip of the Penis for the man or in the testicles for the man. When that person feels that orgasm they will go and pee because the man has blessed the woman with his water, his blessings so automatically the woman would want to go and pee, same with the man also.

In terms of we, as human beings we are not meant to be monogamous but it says in the Bible that God created man and woman and made woman from man's rib but I believe women and men have 24 ribs and out of the 24 ribs, when one man and one woman come together and they become one as the Bible says; The two will become as one. Half of the woman belongs to the man, half of the ribs belong to the woman and man so we potentially have 12 ideals suitable wives or husbands that we can have in our lives in terms of somebody that we can marry and some of us are not meant to be monogamous some of us are polygamous especially in Africa and some parts of the US. You can for example be married to Adwoa and also love Abena, but because of the marriage bond that you may have with each other, you cannot go outside of your marriage but God allows that if you love somebody and that person is a potential spouse you can speak through your wife to that person. You just say the person's name and say sleep (Adwoa) and say wake up (Abena) the other person's name in the persons you are with, will wake up in that person, and you can talk to that person that you love. God allows you to spiritually to speak to that person that you love and even have intercourse with God's permission. Ask for permission from the person and through GOD and THE HOLY SPIRIT, when he or she agrees, you may have consensual intercourse, if it be the WILL OF GOD. It depends on God if he allows you to have children with that person through the person whom you're married with spiritually that onus is on God and if he allows it, but you may ask if you want to an if he permits it shall be done for you so you can be with your wife or husband but talk to your other soul, rib, ideal, true, mate that maybe be with someone else.

I've talked about how to get truth how to date and find your real , true, ideal, soul, spirit, rib mate and now I'm going to talk about hearing the voice of God and doing what he says. In the Bible, it talks about many people who have heard the voice of God in their lives and how God bless them when they availed themselves, listened to God, obeyed God, and finally a reward was given to them. In African spirituality though I have not come across someone admitting that they have heard the voice of God but I believe me, Gloria I have heard the voice of God, because I will use the example of me coming to Canada at a young age. While I was in school, I had a dream that I would travel to Canada in 1995; yes, in every in household in Ghana if somebody's parents is abroad, they automatically assume that they will go abroad, but how did I know specifically that in 1995 is when I'll go and truth be told in 1995 is when I came to Canada. So, I believe God through spiritual means through the ancestor's knowledge, speaks to us with God's permission through the Holy Spirit to see our future. So that is how I believe God spoke to me through the ancestors I believe the creator also gave us the ability and the knowledge of free will. I will start with a story to let you understand what it is I'm trying to convey; a young man searched far and wide and could not find anything to eat during a great famine. He finally found the nut of a palm kernel he tried to break it and it and went down the hole. When the nut of the palm kernel rolled down the hole, the boy followed suit. When he followed the nut, it went into an old ladies dwelling. He found a place filled with lots of different foods, all sorts of foods, all varieties of food, his eyes became very excited because he had hungered for long. As he was wandering and searching the place an old woman came out and asked "who is there? what are you doing here? and what do you want?" he answered "Nana please, I mean no harm to you but there's a famine in my town and I found the nut and I tried to break it but it rolled down your hole so I followed suit." The old woman asked him "what would you like to drink? I have some water, would you

like it?" he drank the water then she asked "what would you like for me to do for you?" he replied "I would like some food" the woman told him to go to a blue room and follow my instructions whatever I say, do it. The boy said "OK" the old woman told him when you go into the blue room there'll be lots of food some will say "pick me, pick me" some will say "don't pick me don't pick me" the one that says pick me please, don't pick it. the one that says "don't pick me" that's the one you should pick. The man went and saw lots of food and the one that said "pick me pick me" was salacious, delicious looking, just everything that he could want and the one that says don't pick me was dirty, almost spoilt, tattered not good-looking, not appealing to him for him to want to taste, so he picked the one that said "pick me" and he went and the lady asked him did you do as I asked you to do he said "yes" then the old lady says "OK" then peel their food that you've gotten and throw away the food and keep the peelings to cook. He thought why "Why would I throw away the perfectly good food and just bold the peelings is this lady OK?", doubt had started to creep in his mind so he did as he pleased. When he finished the food he was cooking, all that

he got was rocks because he didn't follow the directions that the old lady had set for him. In this life we must follow the directions of God, yes, he's given us free will but we need to follow his directions to be able to have a good, honest, good livingof life, so if we behave like this young man did, we will end up with nothing in life but if we follow God's directions with the gift of free will, we will have everlasting enjoyment.

In the African spiritualism when someone insults or says something bad about someone The Holy Spirit with combination of God's will and power allows you to be that person whom you wrong or insulted for a day for you to know why that person is who they are, why they are, how come they become the way they have become. So next time when you see that person or you see something that you don't understand you think twice about what you say. Example if someone gives you wrong information about someone and you act wrongly towards that person the information was given to you about it is not your fault. It is the person who fed you the wrong information's fault and therefore whatever punishment that was supposed to be yours, goes to that person that fed you the wrong information. At times we may do things to someone that we do not remember. But in our lives God reminds us in our own ways and we are supposed to apologize to that person. if you know where that person is contact that person say your name the reason why you're calling, the mistake that you did against them and apologize but if you don't know where that person is anymore, let GOD, through the Holy Spirit through the winds, tell that person that you're sorry and that you hope he or she has a good life and for anything that you've caused him or her to go through, you apologize for and ask for forgiveness and you can do this through God and the Holy Spirit and through whichever prophets that you pray through, ie Muhammad ,Jesus Christ, the son of GOD, because I believe we are all children of God and so It says in Galatians Ch. 3 vs. 26;

"for year all the children of God by faith in Jesus Christ" so since we are all children of God we can ask God our father to help us when we need help, and he will remind us of our faults, but we must rectify the mistakes before he can bless us. For it says in first Corinthians ch. 3 vs. 16 it says "do you not know that you are a temple of God and that the spirit of God dwells in you" so I believe that God's SPIRIT dwells in us and when we ask him and want to do something, he will do it for you. For you need to awaken the GOD in you, and he (GOD) , will help you.

FAIRNESS-

 When God blesses you and others take your blessing You can ask God to see who is doing it and since they take your blessings they should also take your defeats your failures your deaths basically anything that is supposed to happen to you, if the person stole it from you, they're supposed to get the bad. Because with the good

comes the bad also, so whatever good they have taken from you,

they are also to take the bad as well. You can ask this through

whatever prophet that you pray through and with the Holy Spirit

and with God's permission.

<u>SANKOFA-</u>

The creator gave us the ability to fix issues or problems that we might have hurt someone. Sankofa we do not teach it is something that God has to impart on you, so all I can say about SANKOFA is, God gives you the ability to fix the issues that you've done that has caused harm to someone hopefully it didn't hurt the person to the soul because once it's etched in the soul, it's hard to erase it from the soul, only GOD can, so You can ask GOD the directions you must follow for the damage caused to be erased from said person's soul. But whatever monetary issues that there is, you must pay back to the person because that person might still be paying that. Once you're able to fix that person's problem, if God gives you the ability to go back to fix it, do not steal the person's intellectual ability, do not steal anybody's intellectual stuff because that is basically stealing so if you've been given the chance to do SANKOFA don't steal people's ideas.

<u>MENSA AKA, MENSA W) MU/ MA NO NK).</u>

In the past and even now those that do remember it still do it in Ghana and even outside of Ghana if they are descendants of Ghanaians. There is something called inviting somebody to eat once you start eating. You're supposed to pray before eating. I was taught this prayer by Right Reverend Bishop Festus Yeboah-Asuamah "bless the food or Lord my God, be present at my table or Lord my God," You can you invite somebody to eat. Once you invite the person, the person is supposed to deny that they will eat or they will say "their hands are in there"/ they are not physically supposed to eat with you but through the Holy Spirit and through God if the person is hungry if they say "ma no nko" it means let it go they will not be fed. bt if they are hungry they will be fed spiritually and it'll Curb their hunger.

That prayer was taught to me by my mother's sisters husband who is a Bishop of SUNYANI and he's married to my auntie Felicia Yeboah- Asuamah, who is a mother superior. I added on this "remove any impurities that has been placed in this food and let it be used for sustenance, health, growth, nutrition, and to feed those that are hungry and to curb their hunger through the Holy Spirit by God's will let it be done." He also taught me this song "thank you father world so sweet, thank you for the food we eat, thank you for the birds that sing, thank you LORD for everything."

<u>IF IT DOESN'T PAIN OR HURT YOU, THEY WILL NOT</u>

<u>STOP/ STOP IT FOR YOU WILL NOT LIKE IT IF IT IS</u>

<u>DONE TO YOU.-</u>

There are people that like to put blockages, hinders, stoppages in people's lives. they do it spiritually, they do it physically ,through gossip through false information and in the AKAN culture they say if it is done to you and you do not complain or it doesn't hurt you, they will keep on doing it but I have a saying that, if it is done to you, will not like it so, stop it.

ABOUT THE AUTHOR

I am a mom of a wonderful son, whom GOD gifted me. I am married to Edward Asamoah Frimpong, who is a wonderful man and I am blessed with a generous, GOD LOVING, FEARING, HONEST INDIVIDUALS AS FAMILY MEMBERS AND FRIENDS.

I was born in Ghana and emigrated to Canada when I was 11 years old. I have lived in Canada for 26 with some vacation times, going back to GHANA.

I love both Countries and the BLESSINGS they've been in my life.

www.ingramcontent.com/pod-product-compliance
Lightning Source LLC
Chambersburg PA
CBHW051405150726
48000CB00003B/1339